THE FLOWERS WILL BLOOM
THE CRITTERS WILL CRAWL
TO NATURES FINE TUNE
THE LIGHT GATHERS ALL

TIME THAT'S WELL SPENT
WILL HELP CALM THE SOUL
& LOVE THAT IS MEANT
WILL MAKE YOU FEEL WHOLE

DON'T TRY TO FIT IN
YOU'LL FIND TRUTH OUTSIDE THE PACK
BUT IF YOU FOLLOW ALONG
THE MORE SKILLS YOU'LL TEND TO LACK

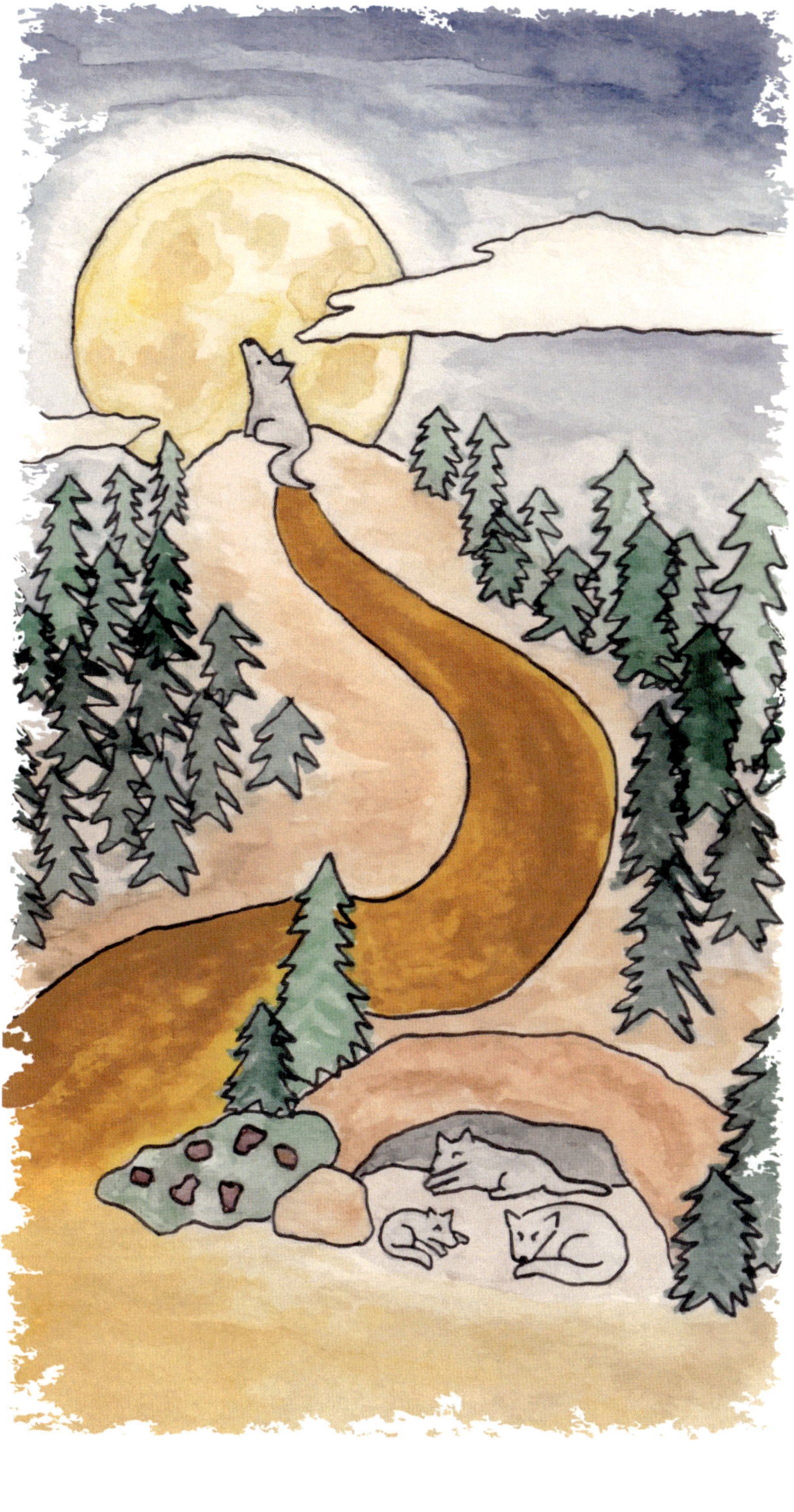

POSITIVE, POSITIVE
IF SUCCESS IS WHAT YOU THINK
THEN ALL YOUR DREAMS AND WONDERS
WILL COME TRUE IN JUST A BLINK

THOUGH WE MIGHT BE DIFFERENT
THE KEY IS JUST TO LOVE
NO, HATE IS NOT THE ANSWER
IN A WORLD THAT WE'RE PROUD OF

A LIFE THAT'S BUILT ON SAND
IT WILL SURELY RISE & FALL
LOOK FOR WHAT IS STEADY
SO YOUR MIND WILL WITHSTAND ALL

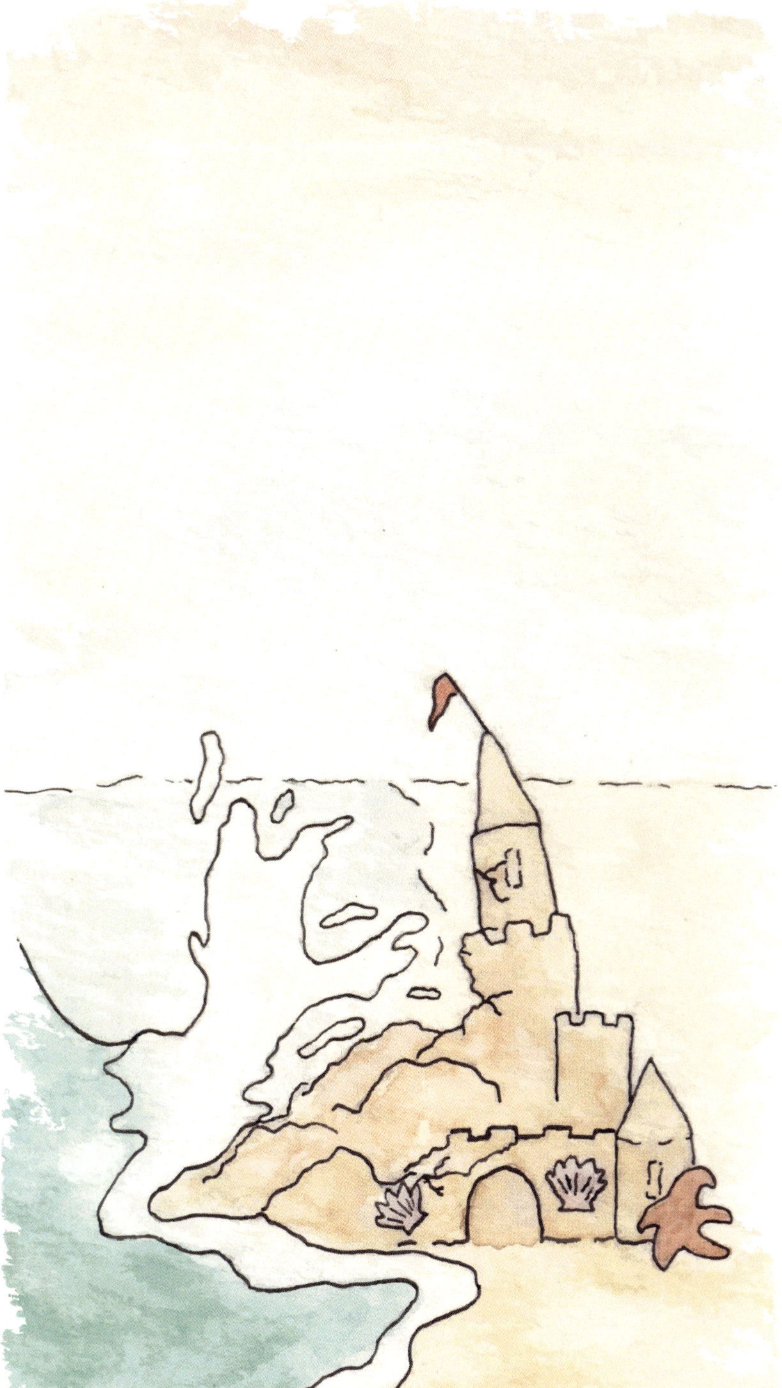

NO MATTER WHERE YOU START
YOU CONTROL THE END
DON'T YOU EVER FEEL ALONE
YOUR MIND CAN BE YOUR FRIEND

THE WAY TO CONQUER FEAR
RUN AT IT WITH FULL FORCE
AS ALL YOUR PROBLEMS FADE
YOU'LL WATCH THEM RUN THEIR COURSE

TRUST IN YOUR WINGS
BELIEVE YOU CAN FLY
GO AFTER YOUR DREAMS
DON'T LET LIFE PASS YOU BY

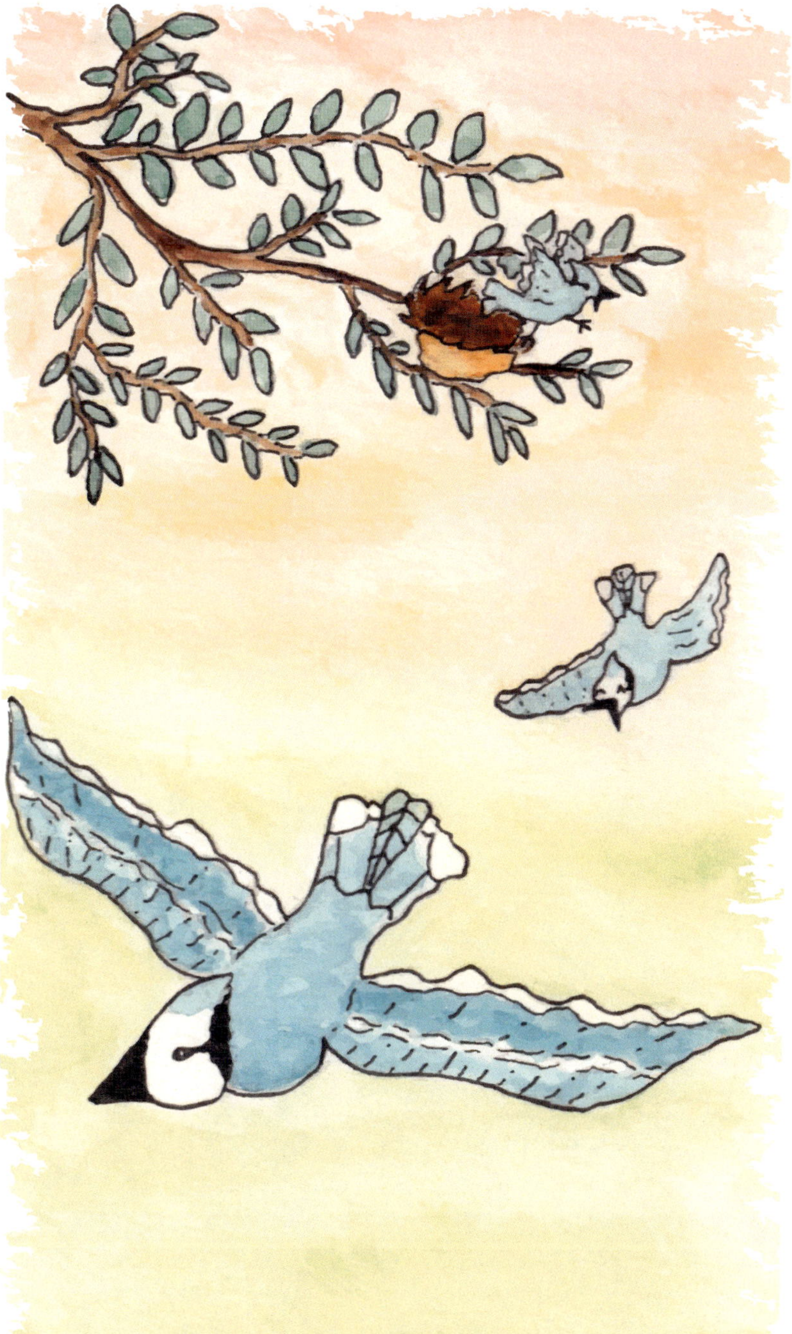

WHEN YOU FOCUS ON PAIN
THERE'S NOTHING TO GAIN
THE WAY TO CHEER UP
IS TO TAKE OFF THE CHAIN

IF YOU'RE LOST DON'T FREAK OUT
IT WON'T WORK IF YOU DOUBT
FOR ONE DAY THE WAY
IN YOUR MIND WILL SPROUT

THE BUTTERFLY FLIES
BUT BEFORE, IT JUST CRAWLED
SO JUST TAKE YOUR TIME
BECAUSE SOON YOU'LL BE CALLED

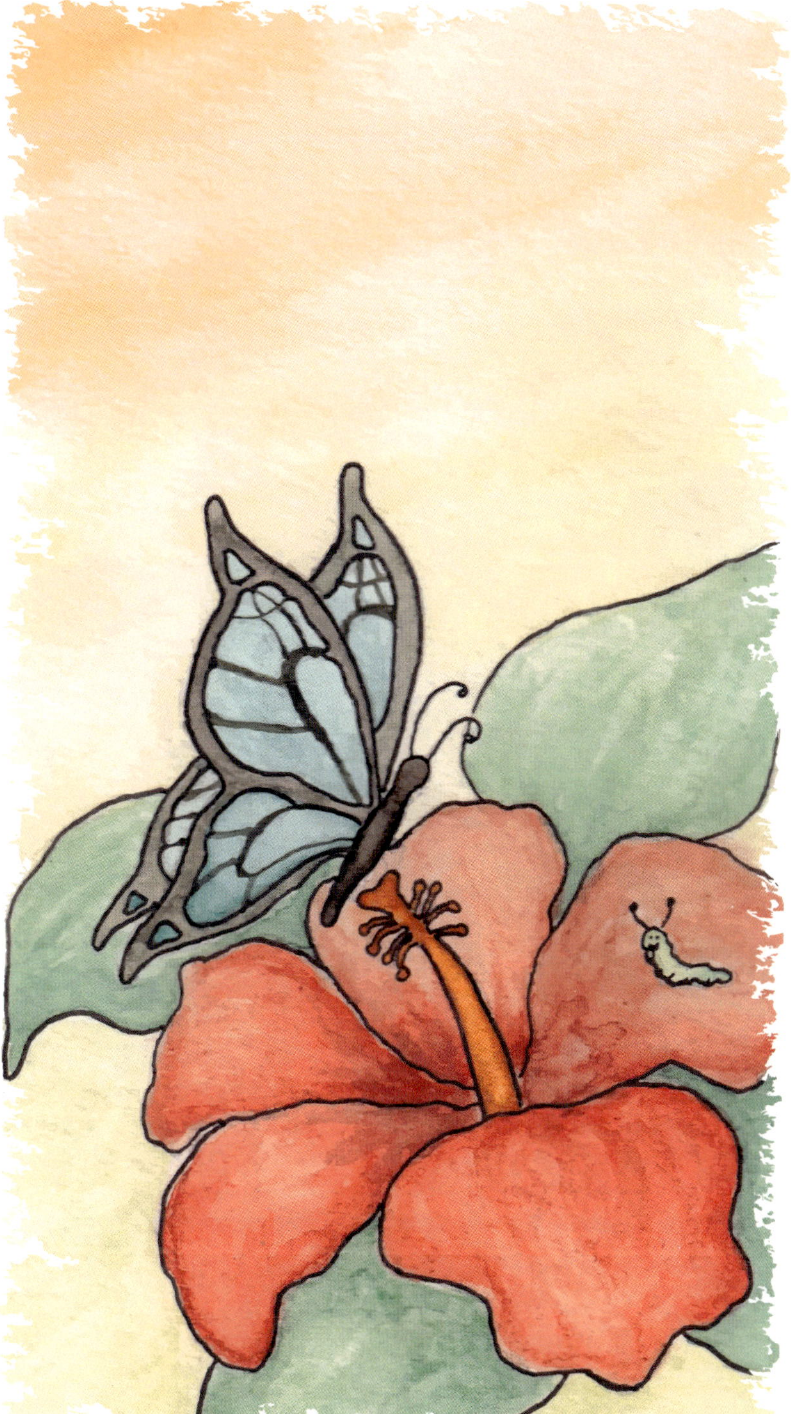

SATISFIED WITH LITTLE
NOW THIS IS THE TRICK
TO KEEP FAR AWAY
FROM JEALOUSY'S PRICK

YOU MUST THINK YOU ARE STRONG
TO GET THROUGH THE PAIN
IN A WORLD FULL OF LIES
THERE'S STILL TRUTH TO GAIN

NO NEED TO COMPARE
YOU'RE ALREADY GOOD ENOUGH
IT'S GOOD TO BE DIFFERENT
YOU MUST STRIVE TO BE TOUGH

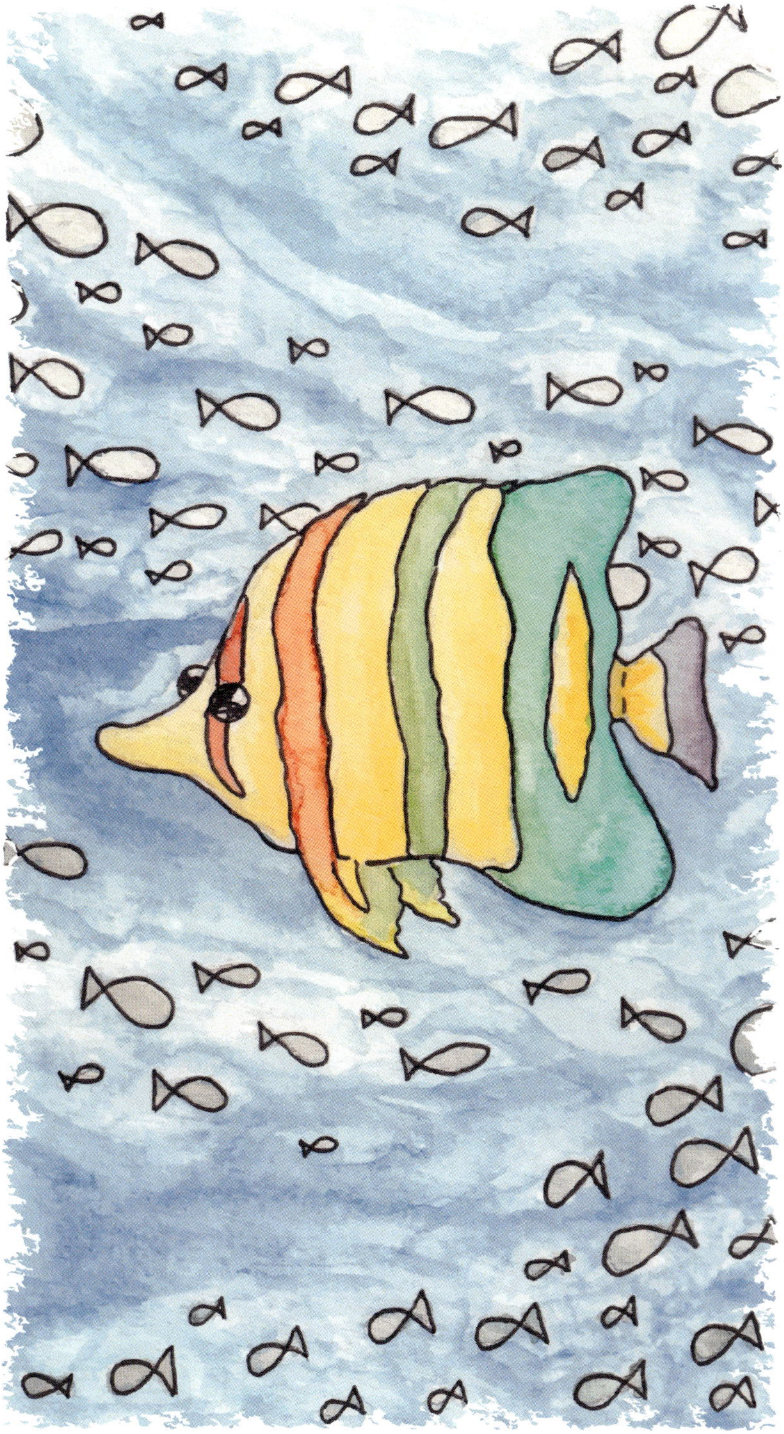

GOOD THINGS WILL COME
TO THOSE WHO CAN FEEL
ONCE STARTED AS THOUGHT
& THEN BECAME REAL

BECOME LIKE A SEED
FIGURE OUT WHAT YOU NEED
SO THAT EVEN IN DROUGHT
YOUR MIND CAN STAY FREED

MAKE LIKE A BEE
BE AS SWEET AS SOME HONEY
THE GOODNESS YOU SEE
SO THAT LIFE'S ALWAYS SUNNY

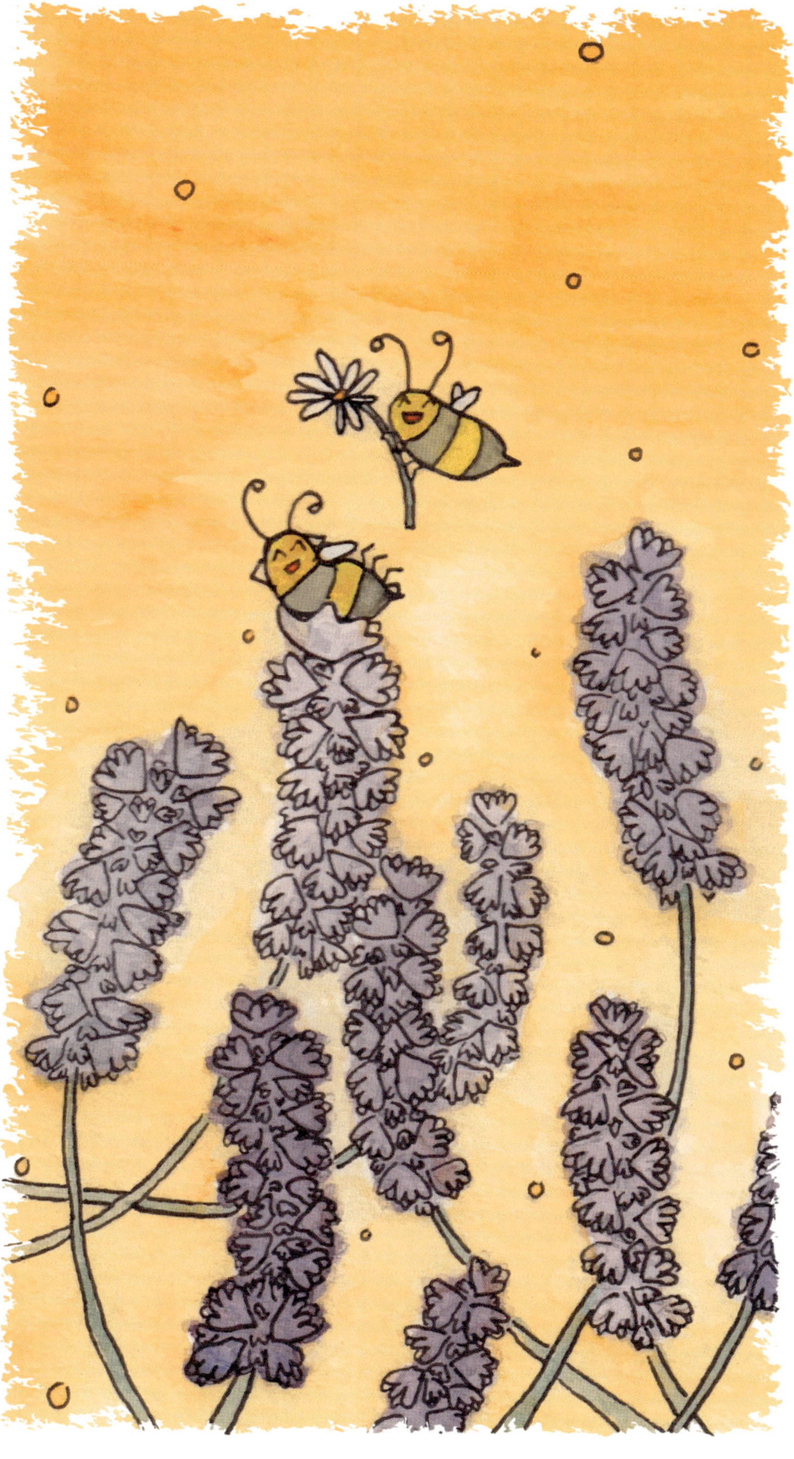

NATURE BRINGS US LIFE
SO STEP OUT IN HER BEAUTY
SHE'S THE ONE SIMPLE CURE
WHEN YOU'RE DOWN OR FEELING MOODY

THOUGHTS DESTROY THE MIND
DESIRES WITHER THE HEART
LIKE A PLANT WITHOUT SOME WATER
WITHOUT LOVE IT CANNOT START

IN A WORLD OF ENERGY
WE MUST DO WHAT IS RIGHT
WHEN WE DO WHAT IS WRONG
WE'RE JUST DIMMING OUR LIGHT

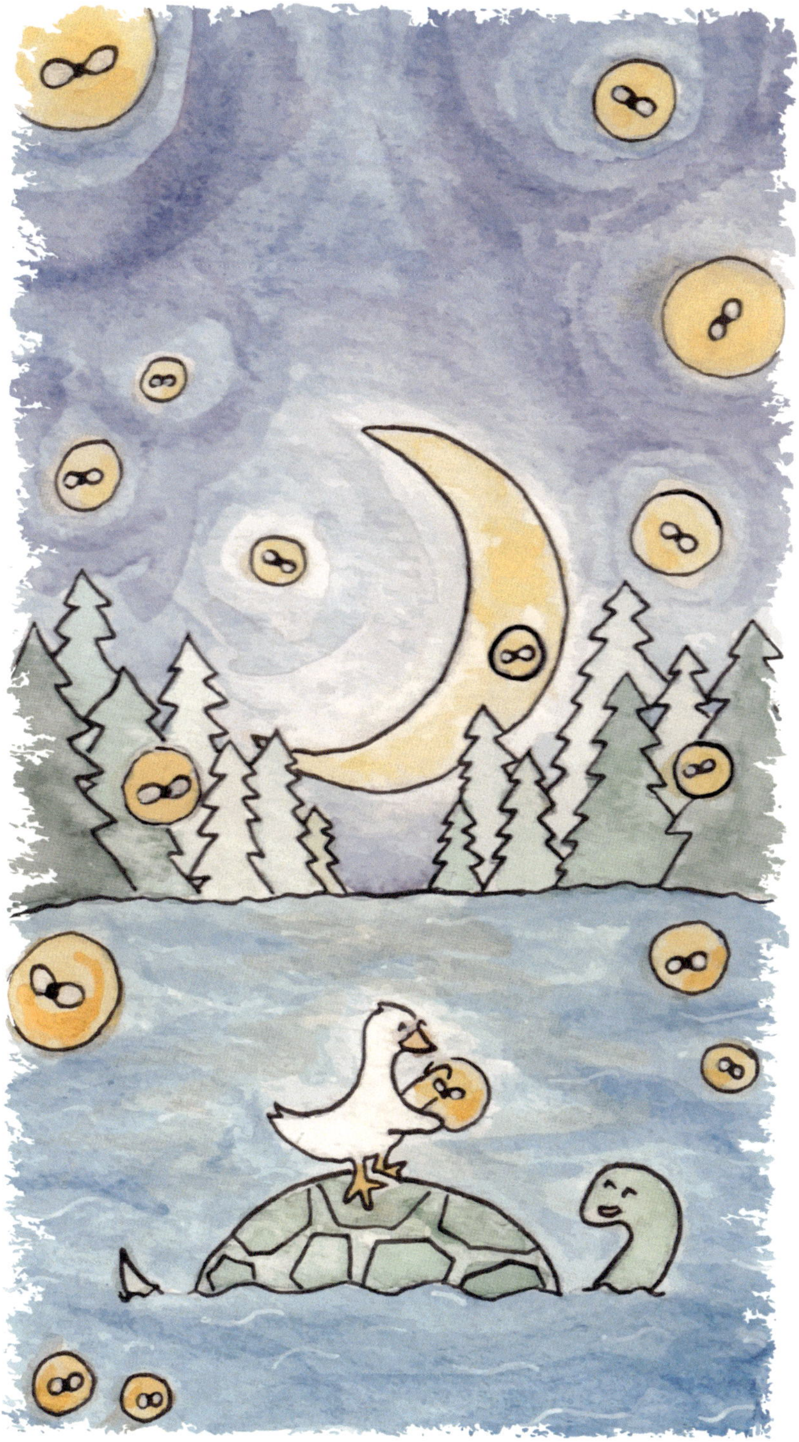

YOUR BRAIN IS LIKE A MUSCLE
YOU MUST WORK TO KEEP IT STRONG
NEVER QUIT IN ALL YOUR LEARNING
SO YOUR FUTURE CAN BE LONG

ANYTHING IS POSSIBLE
FOR THE ONE WHO THINKS AND BREATHES
THERE IS A FORCE INSIDE
TO SUPPLY YOU ALL YOUR NEEDS

YOU'LL NEVER BE CONFRONTED
WITH A PROBLEM YOU CAN'T SOLVE
IT'S YOUR CHOICE IF YOU WORRY
OR CONTINUE TO EVOLVE

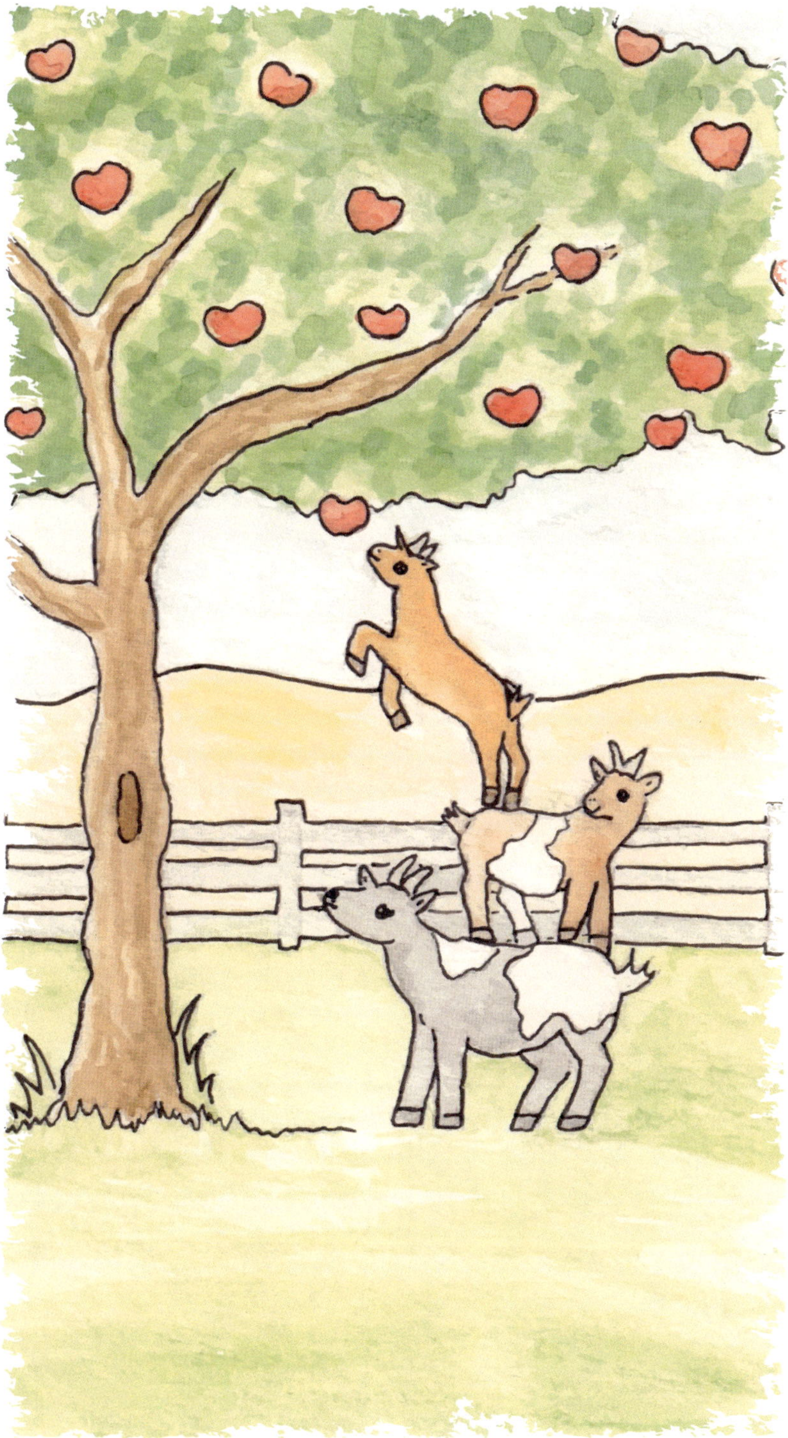

PROBLEMS ARE A CHALLENGE
YOU CAN EITHER STAND OR FALL
DON'T LET THEM BREAK YOU DOWN
YOU MUST BE STRONG & STAND UP TALL

WHAT'S RUNNING THROUGH YOUR HEAD
DOES IT LEAD TO GOOD OR BAD?
YOUR ONLY GOAL SHOULD BE
TO MAKE EVERYONE ELSE FEEL GLAD

THERE'S ALWAYS ROOM TO LAUGH
THERE'S ALWAYS TIME FOR JOY
ALWAYS A CHANCE TO LOVE
& SO MUCH IN LIFE TO ENJOY

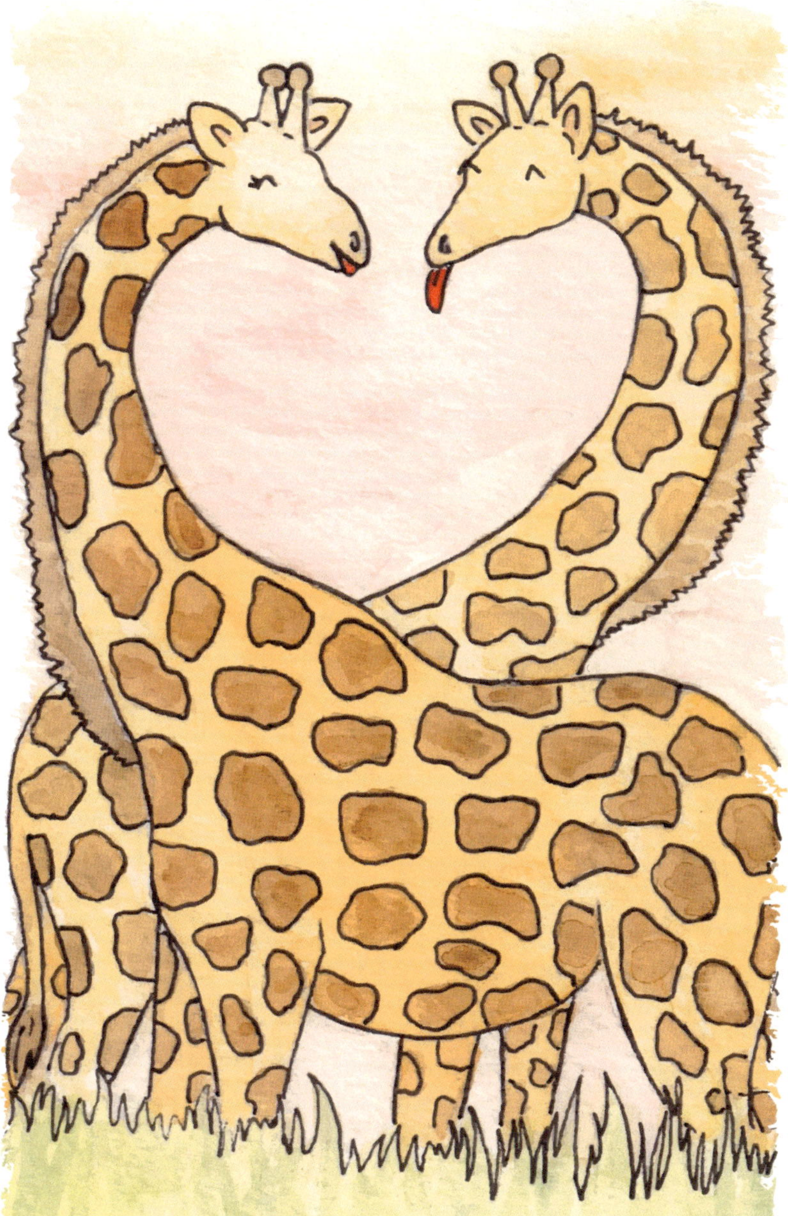

LIKE A SHIP OUT AT SEA
WHERE IT'S OPEN & FREE
LET YOUR BODY ESCAPE
SO THE NEGATIVE WILL FLEE

KEEP YOUR EYES ON THE PRIZE
& YOUR DREAMS IN THE SKIES
LET THIS MESSAGE SOAK IN
SO YOU CAN FOLLOW THE WISE

ABANDONED & ALONE
WHEN FAR AWAY FROM HOME
EVEN THOUGH THERE'S DANGER
HELP COULD COME FROM A STRANGER

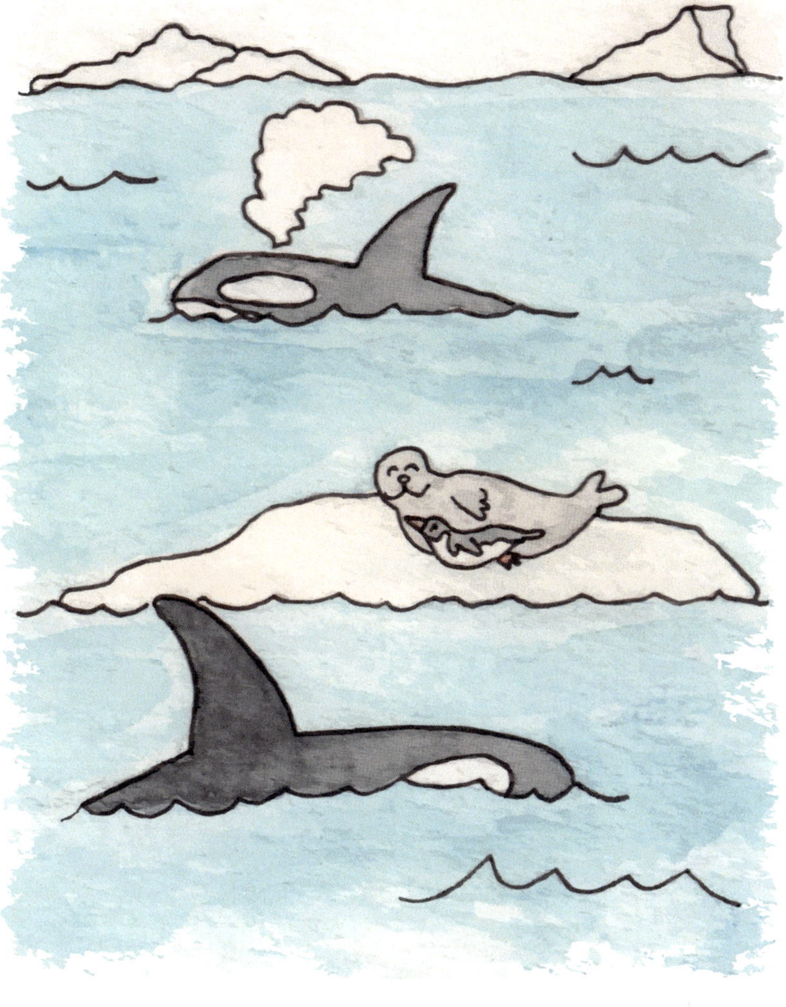

KNOWLEDGE IS NO GOOD
IF IT'S NEVER PUT TO ACTION
BUT IF YOU START TO TRY
THEN YOU'LL FINALLY GET SOME TRACTION

YOU ONLY WILL BECOME
LIKE WHO YOU ARE SURROUNDED
THEY EITHER BUILD OR BREAK
LEAVE YOU EMPTY OR WELL ROUNDED

WHEN ONE THING SEEMS TOO BIG
FIND OTHERS TO ASSIST
ANYTHING IS POSSIBLE
TO THE ONES WHO WILL PERSIST

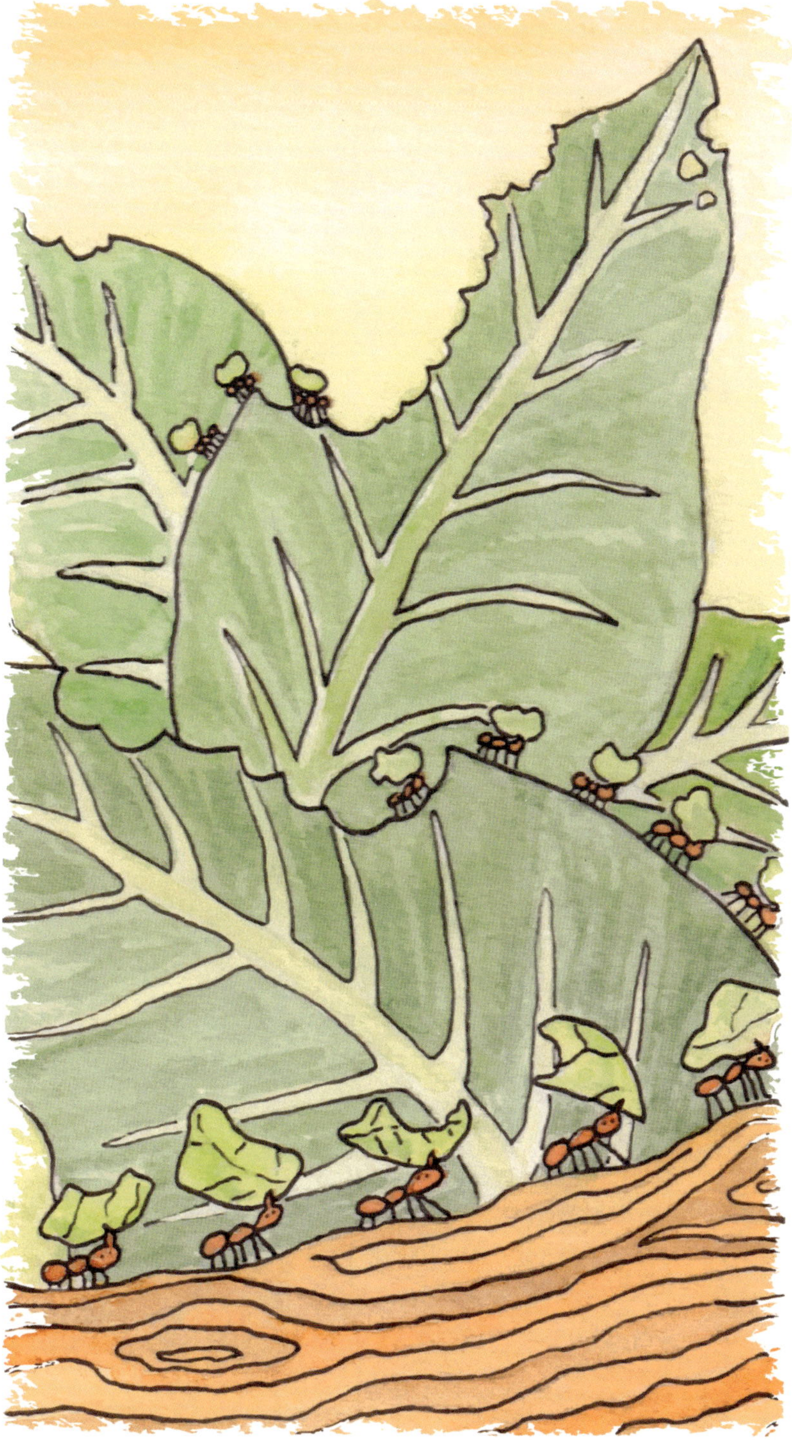

EVEN IF THEY'RE FRIENDLY
THEY COULD ALSO BRING YOU PAIN
THE FRIENDS THAT YOU RELY ON
BE AWARE OF WHAT THEY GAIN

DON'T MIMIC WHAT YOU SEE
OR MIMIC WHAT YOU HEAR
YOU SHOULD ALWAYS BE YOURSELF
SO YOU DON'T END UP IN FEAR

LEARNING TO FIT IN
& BLEND INTO THE SCENE
WILL REALLY ONLY WORK
IF YOU WANT TO BE UNSEEN

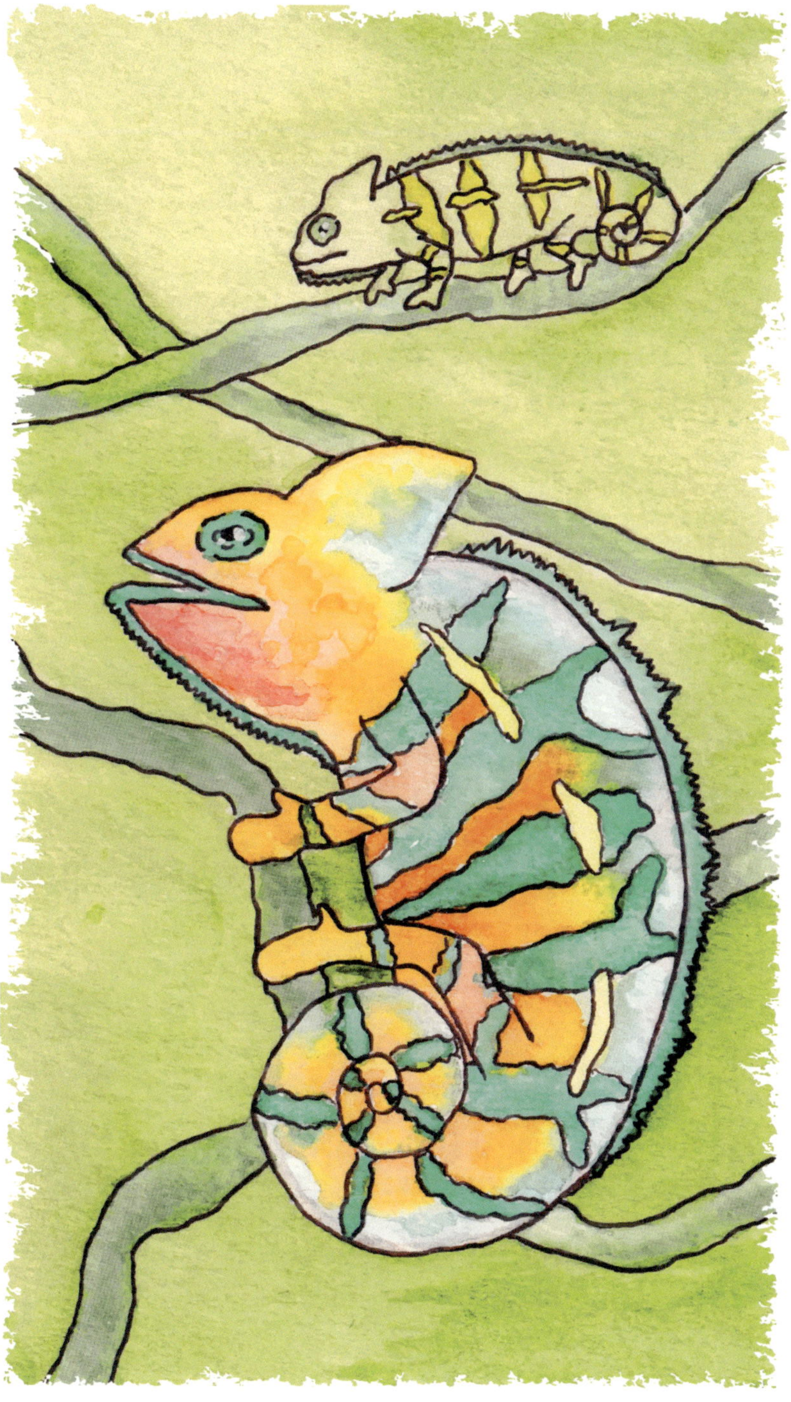

IF YOU'RE WATCHING THE CLOCK
YOU'RE NOT HAPPY WHERE YOU ARE
STOP WASTING ALL YOUR TIME
LIFE'S A MOVIE, BE THE STAR

THE PROBLEMS THAT YOU FACE
ARE THE PROBLEMS THAT YOU CAUSED
IF YOU NEVER BLAME YOURSELF
THEN YOUR GOALS WILL STAY ON PAUSED

YOU'VE GOTTA KEEP THINGS COOL
& STAY OUT OF THE DRAMA
IT'S BETTER TO BE GENTLE
LIKE THE CHILL & FRIENDLY LLAMA

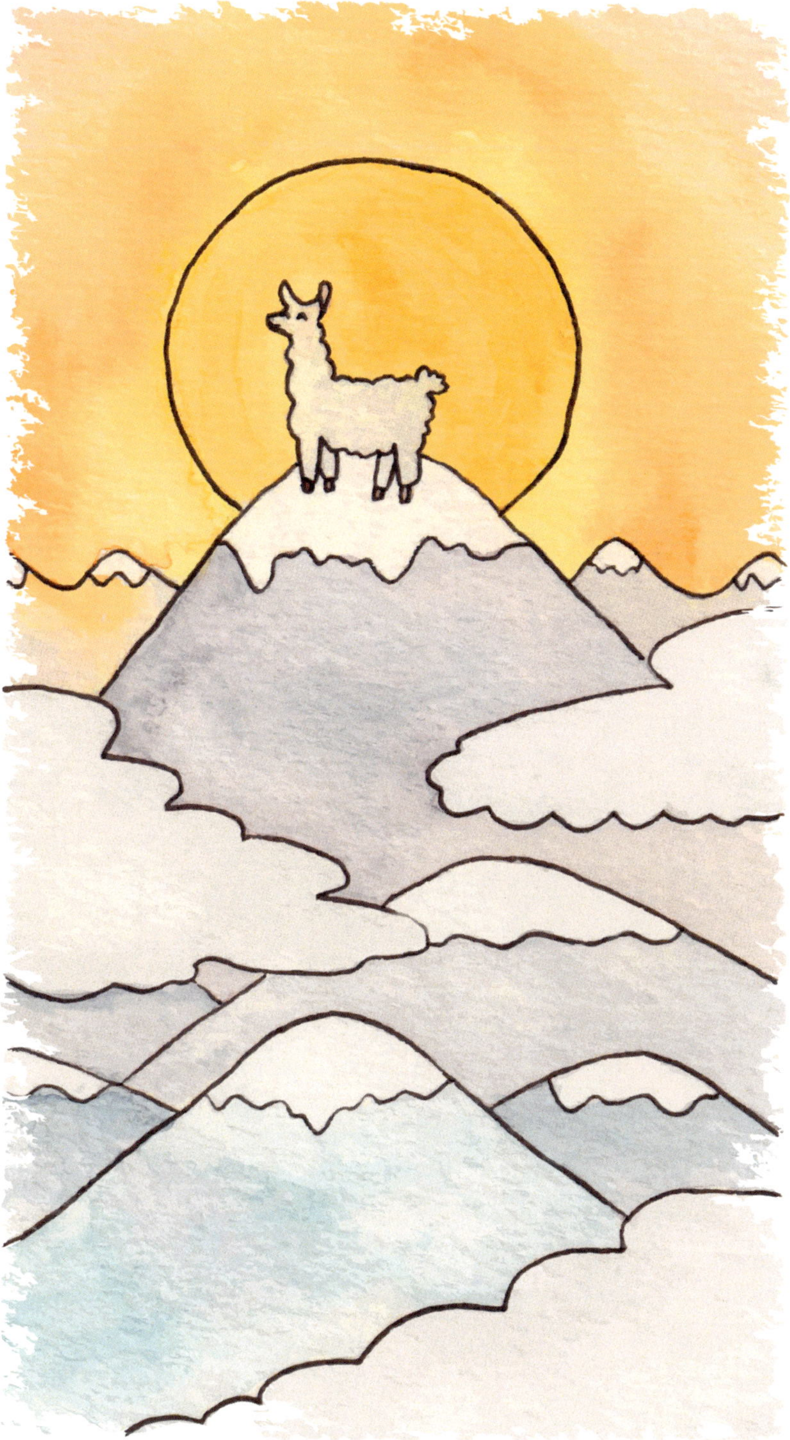

THOUGH IT IS NOT COMFY
DON'T RUN AWAY FROM GROWTH
YOU CAN EITHER STAY THE SAME
OR REALIZE YOU CAN'T HAVE BOTH

WHEN THE TIMES GET HARD
YOU MUST KEEP GOING THROUGH
JUST ON THE OTHER SIDE
IS A MUCH MORE CLEAR VIEW

WHEN THE CURRENT GETS TOO STRONG
HOLD ON WITH ALL YOUR MIGHT
THE STORM WON'T LAST FOREVER
THERE'S NO NEED TO LIVE IN FRIGHT

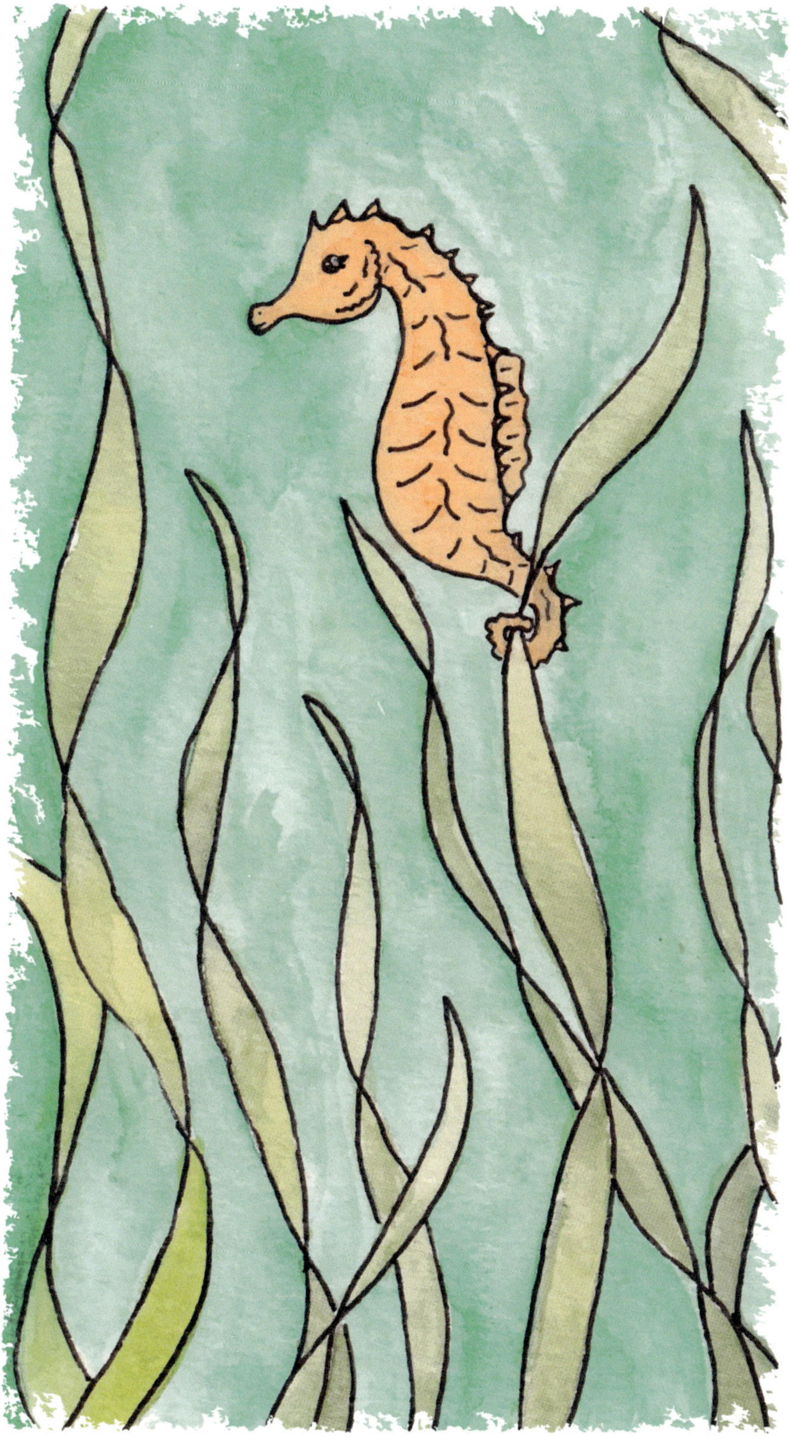

THE ANSWER IS LOVE
IN A WORLD FULL OF HATE
DON'T GO WALKING IN CIRCLES
WHEN THE PATH IS JUST STRAIGHT

THE FOOD THAT YOU EAT
IT WILL BUILD OR DESTROY
IT'S YOUR CHOICE TO MAKE
IF YOU'RE SAD OR FEEL JOY

SUNFLOWERS FULL OF SEEDS
SO PRETTY AND NUTRITIOUS
THE DIET THAT NATURE BREEDS
IS SO HEALTHY AND DELICIOUS

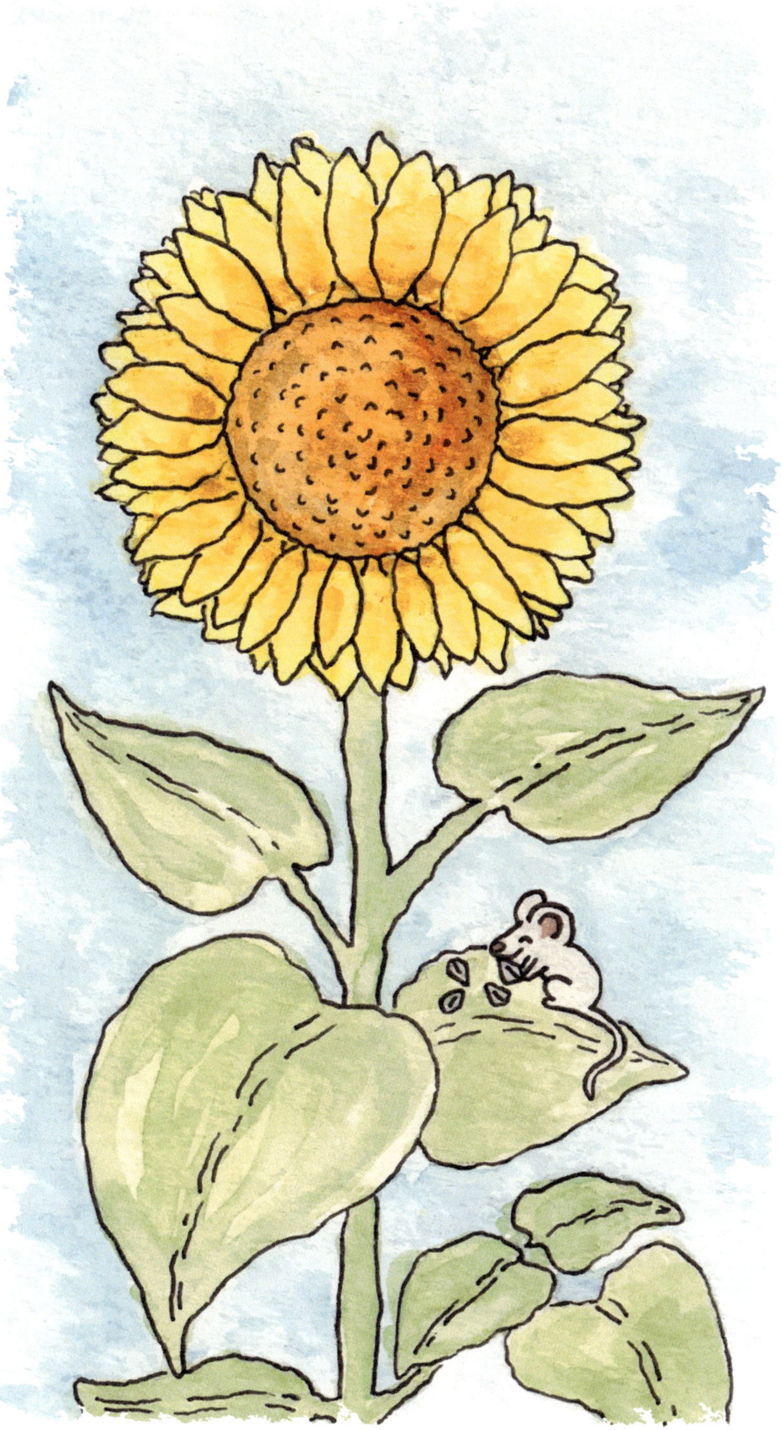

PARENTS DO THEIR BEST
TO GUIDE YOU ON YOUR WAY
& EVEN IF THEY'RE WRONG
PAY ATTENTION TO WHAT THEY SAY

IF YOU KNOW YOUR WORTH
THEN YOU'LL NEVER HAVE TO QUESTION
WHAT THE OTHER PEOPLE THINK
SO JUST FOCUS ON PROGRESSION

WHEN YOU MOVE WITH GRACE
& YOU KEEP A STEADY PACE
REMEMBER TO BE PATIENT
FOR THOSE THINGS YOU WANT TO CHASE

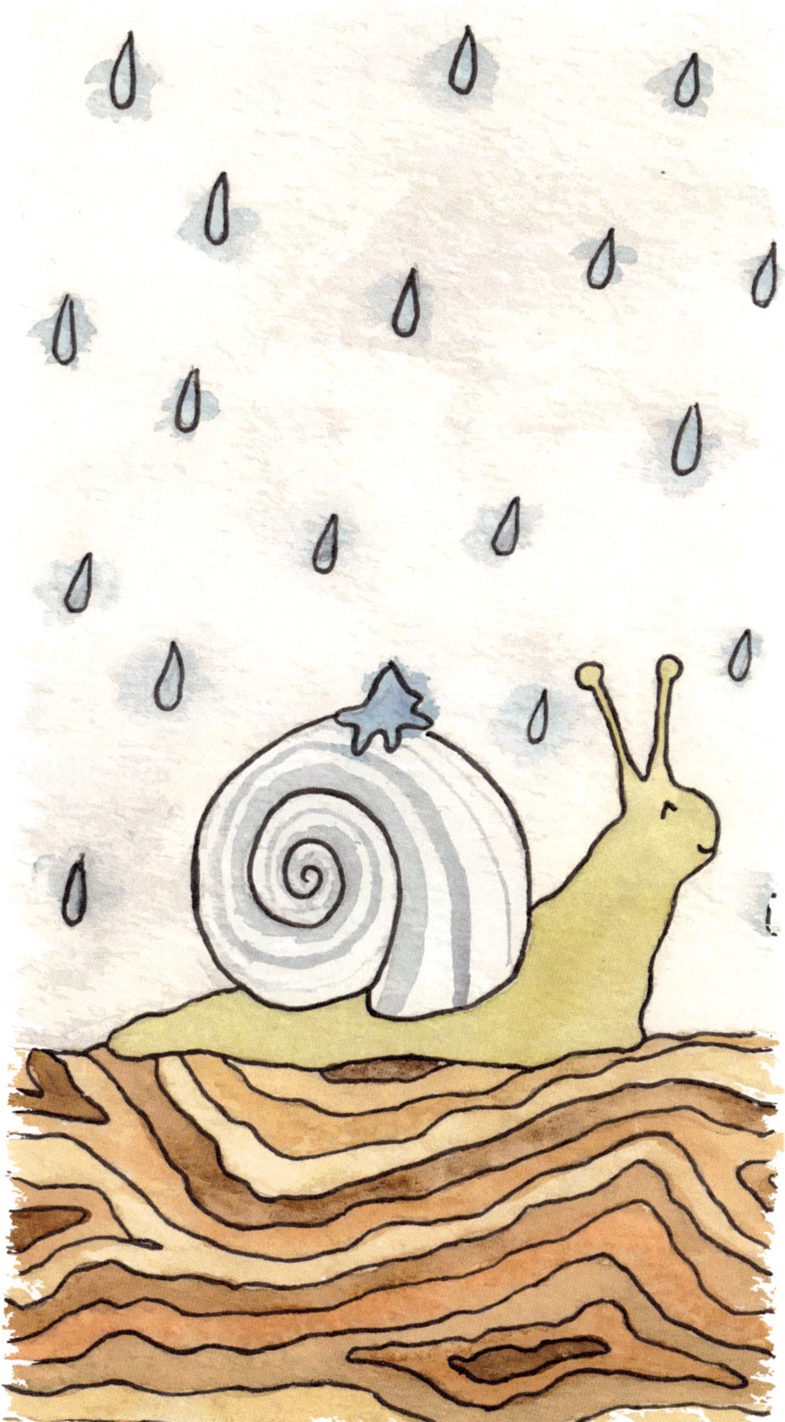

LIFE IS FOR THE LIVING
THE GRAVE IS FOR THE DEAD
IT'S UNDER YOUR CONTROL
THE THOUGHTS RUNNING IN YOUR HEAD

FOCUS ON ABUNDANCE
& DO NOT LOOK FOR LACK
IT'S ALL ABOUT PERSPECTIVE
& IF SO, YOU'LL FIND YOUR TRACK

WE WERE SPECIALLY DESIGNED
SO WE COULD GROW & TO THRIVE
NO MATTER THE CONDITIONS
WE KEEP THE THIRST TO SURVIVE

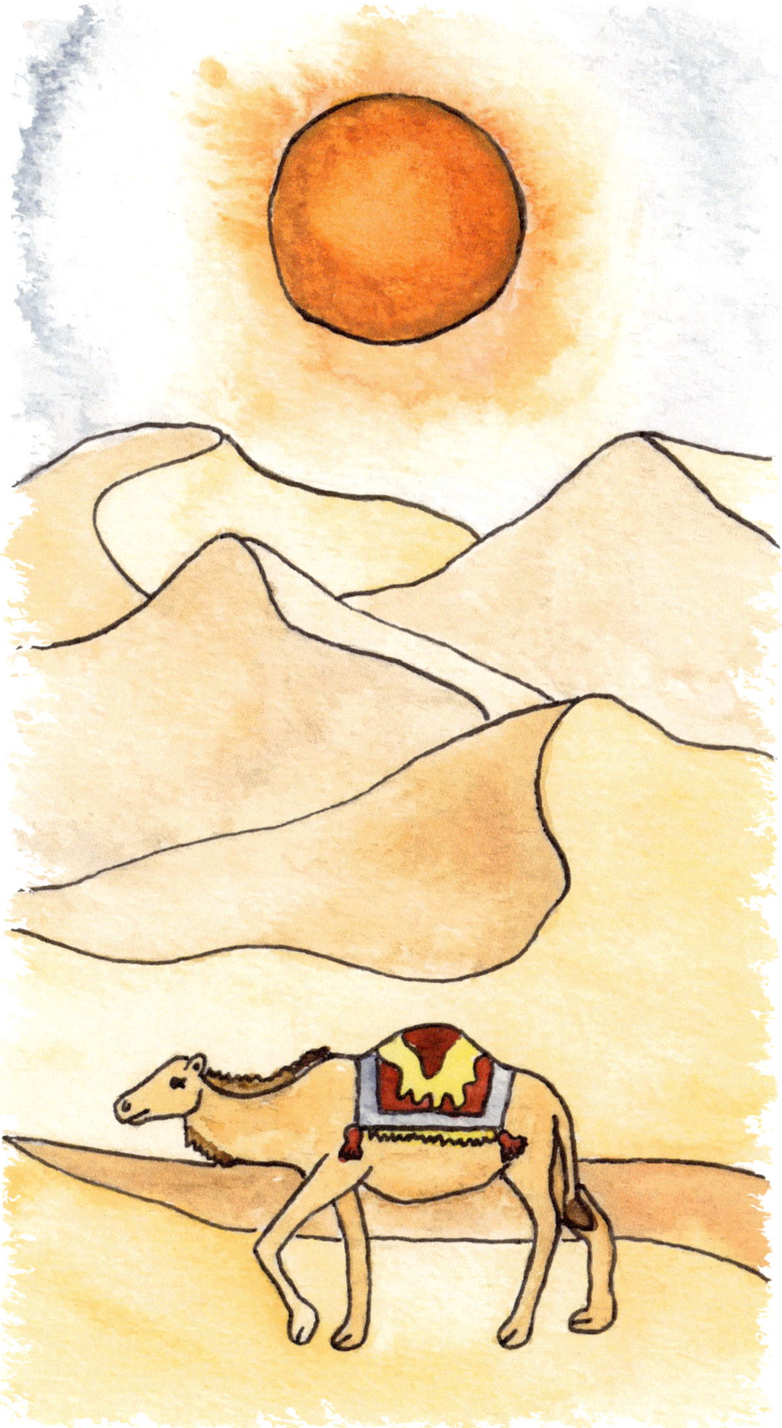

SELF-CONFIDENCE THE WAY
DON'T YOU EVER GO ASTRAY
IF YOU DON'T HAVE IT YET
THEN DON'T WAIT ANOTHER DAY

WHAT A BEAUTIFUL SIGHT
WHEN DARK TURNS TO LIGHT
LET YOUR THOUGHTS TAKE YOU UP
AS THE WIND TAKES THE KITE

IF YOU WANT TO PLAY AT NIGHT
MAKE SURE THAT YOU CAN SEE
FOR IT'S A DIFFERENT WORLD
IF YOUR MIND IS TRULY FREE

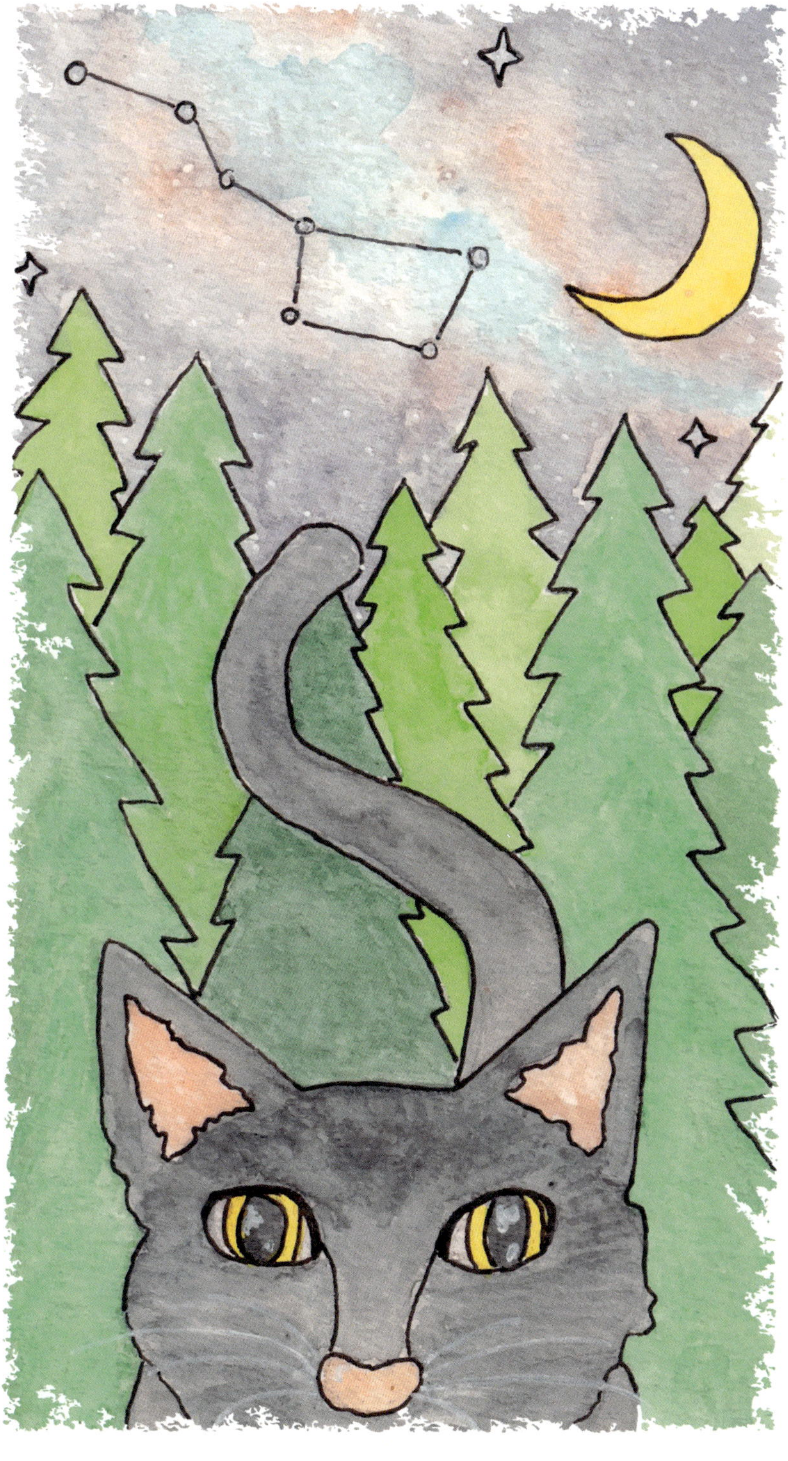

YOUR MIND IS DIVINE
LEAVE THE EVIL BEHIND
YOU'LL KNOW WHEN YOU FEEL
THAT THERE'S TRUE LOVE THAT'S REAL

TRY NOT ARGUE
OR ALWAYS BE RIGHT
WE'RE IN THIS TOGETHER
IN SEARCH OF SOME LIGHT

IF CONFRONTED WITH BAD WORDS
RELY ON YOUR THICK SKIN
STRIVE TO KEEP IT PEACEFUL
SO BOTH SIDES WILL ALWAYS WIN

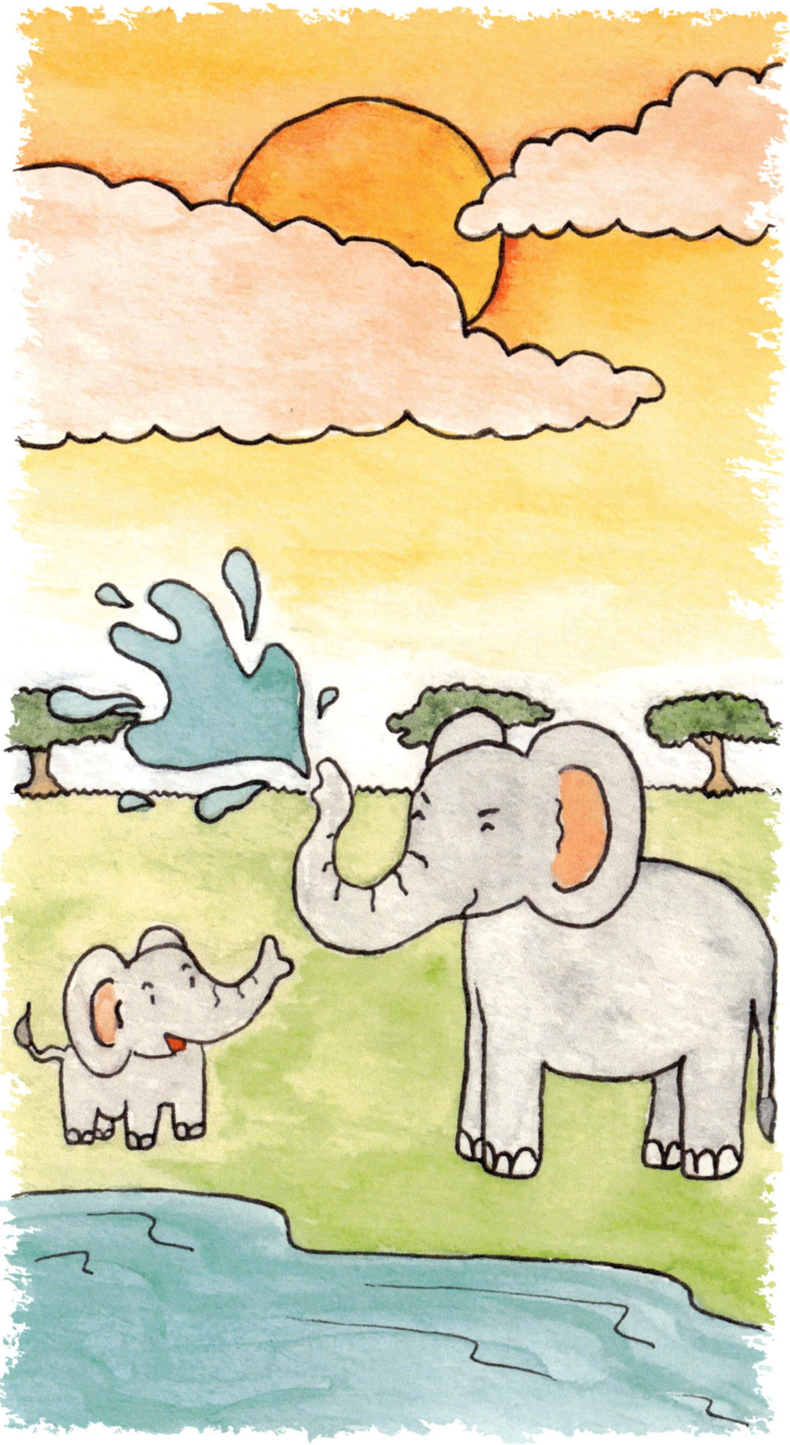

INFORMATION IS FOOD
WHAT WILL YOU FEED YOUR MIND?
WE'LL ALL GET WHAT WE WANT
IN A WORLD WHERE WE'RE ALL KIND

IF YOU ACCEPT YOURSELF
THE WHOLE WORLD FALLS IN LINE
WHEN THERE'S SOMETHING YOU DON'T LIKE
IT WILL NEVER HELP TO WHINE

IF YOU'RE ALWAYS IN A MOOD
IT'LL HAVE YOU FEELING CRABBY
YOU JUST GOTTA LIGHTEN UP
& YOUR LIFE WON'T BE TOO SHABBY

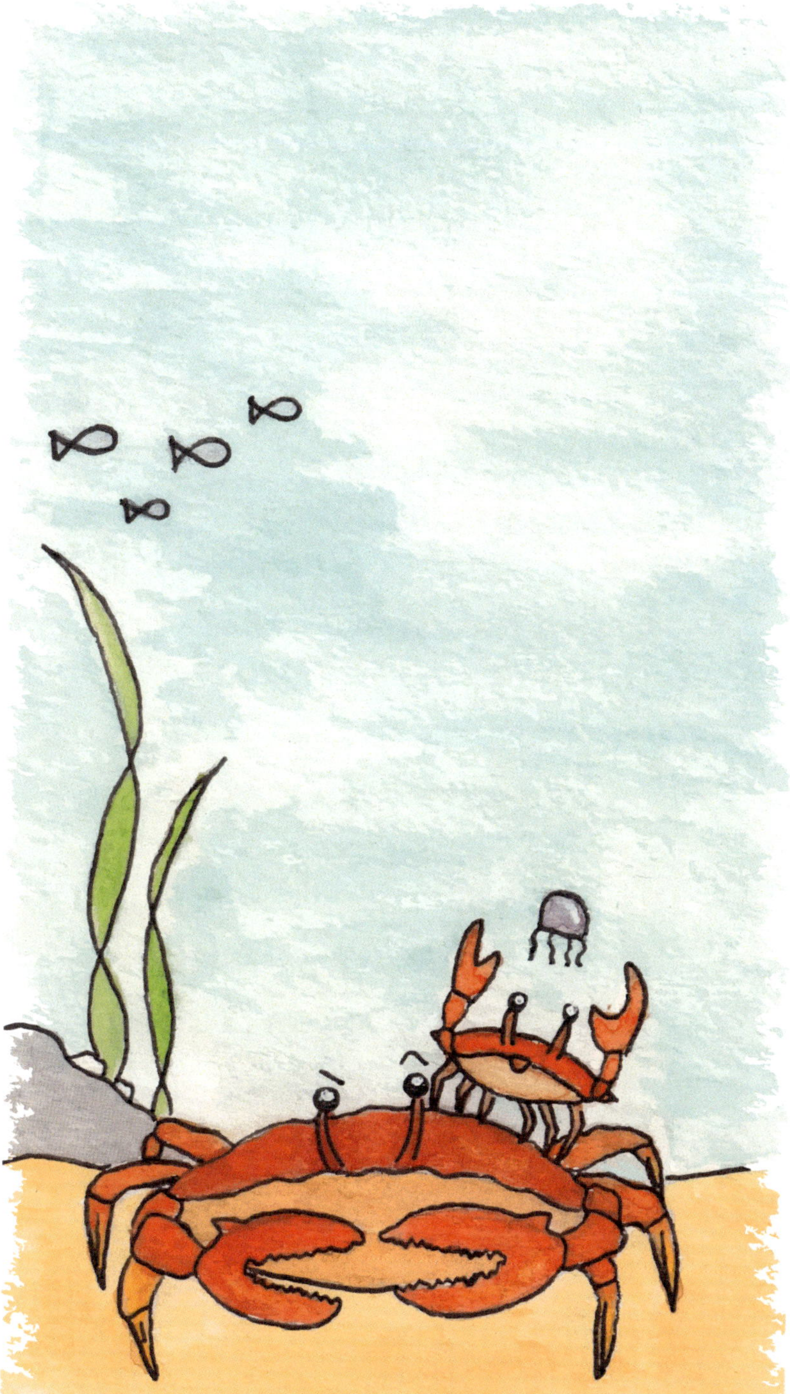

SLAVERY STILL EXISTS
IT EXISTS WITHIN YOUR MIND
DON'T FALL INSIDE THE TRAP
OR YOU'LL END UP FAR BEHIND

LIKE MUSIC TO THE EAR
WE NEED SWEET AND GENTLE
WITH A MINDSET TO SHARE
ON AN EARTH THAT'S OUR RENTAL

ALWAYS STAY CURIOUS
OF THINGS YOU DO NOT KNOW
BUT NEVER TO THE POINT
WHERE MISCHEIF STARTS TO SHOW

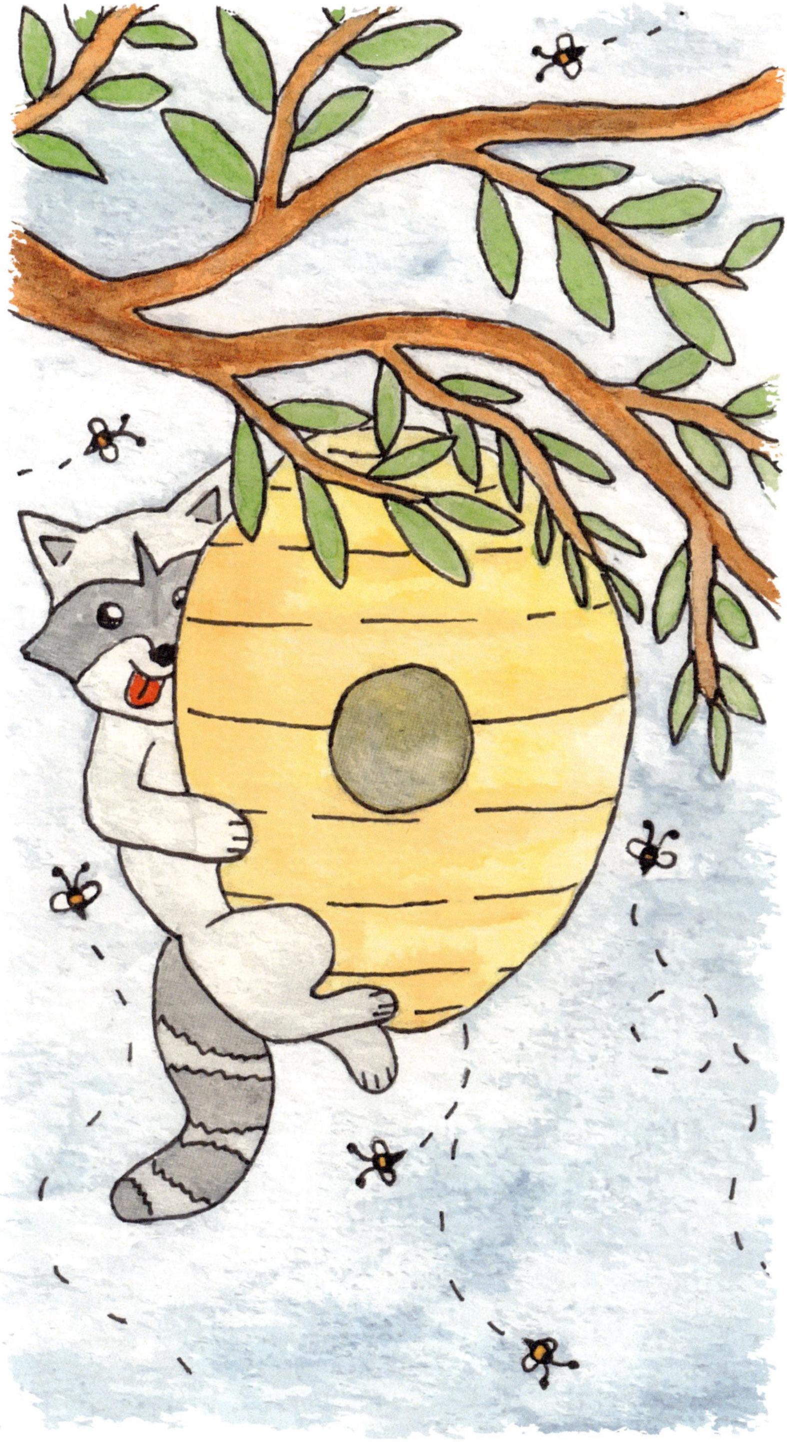

LOSE THE EGO, BUILD YOUR SOUL
THIS IS THE MASTER GOAL
IF YOU LISTEN TO THE VOICE
THEN YOU'LL UNDERSTAND YOUR ROLE

JUST LIKE BLANKETS KEEP US WARM
& THE ROOF WILL HIDE THE STORM
OUR THOUGHTS ARE OUR PROTECTION
FROM OUR MOST UNWANTED FORM

DON'T FOCUS ON THE COVER
IT'S ABOUT WHAT IS INSIDE
A CACTUS IS REAL PRICKLY
BUT ITS FLOWERS NEVER HIDE

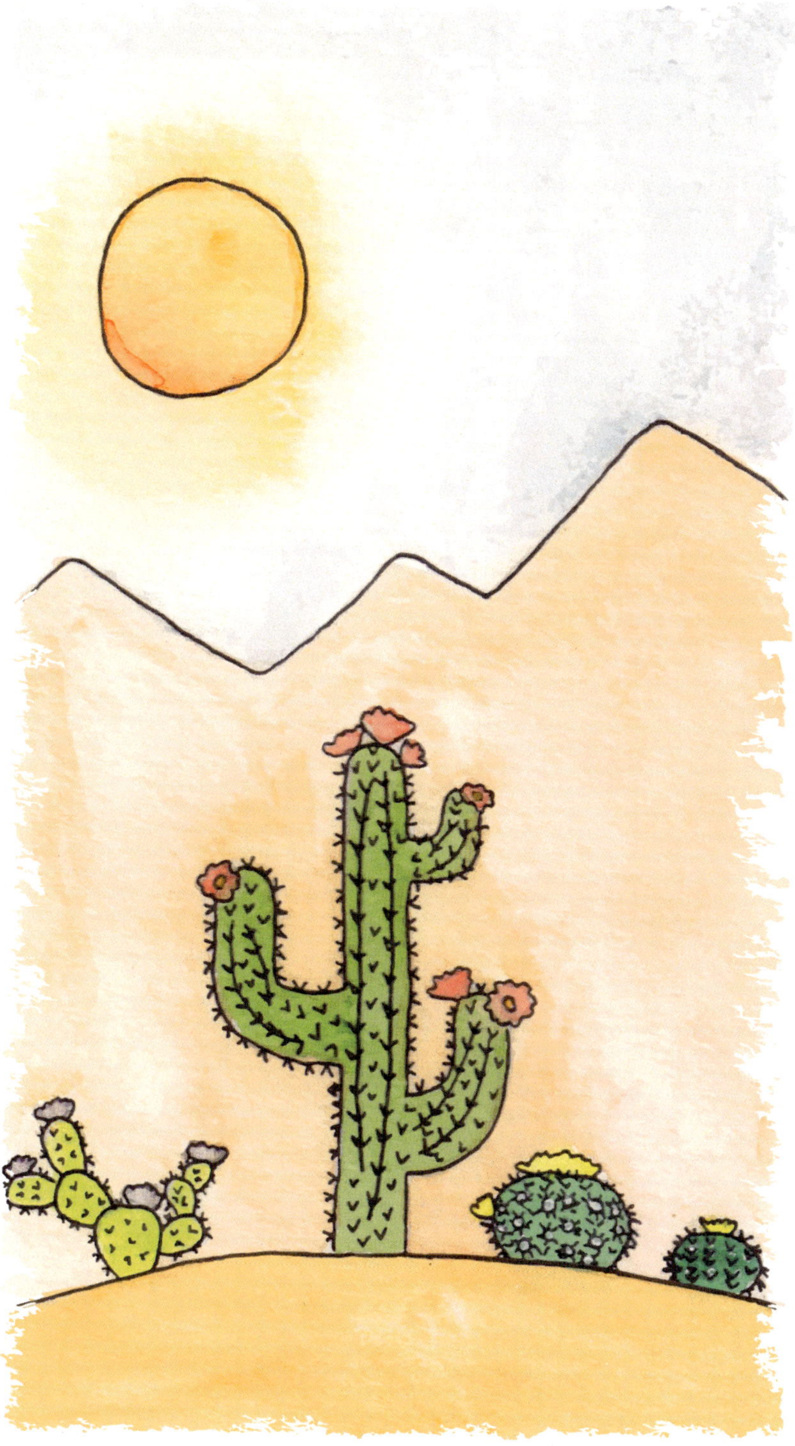

IF YOU DON'T COME OUT ON TOP
YOU HAVEN'T LOST THE WAR
LOSING GIVES US LESSONS
THAT AREN'T EASY TO IGNORE

BE GRATEFUL WITH WHAT YOU HAVE
IT COULD ALWAYS BE MUCH WORSE
COMPARING YOURSELF TO OTHERS
ONLY ENDS UP AS A CURSE

SURVIVAL IS A MUST
NO MATTER THE CONDITION
IF THE CURRENT IS TOO STRONG
IT CAN LEAD TO MORE FRUITION

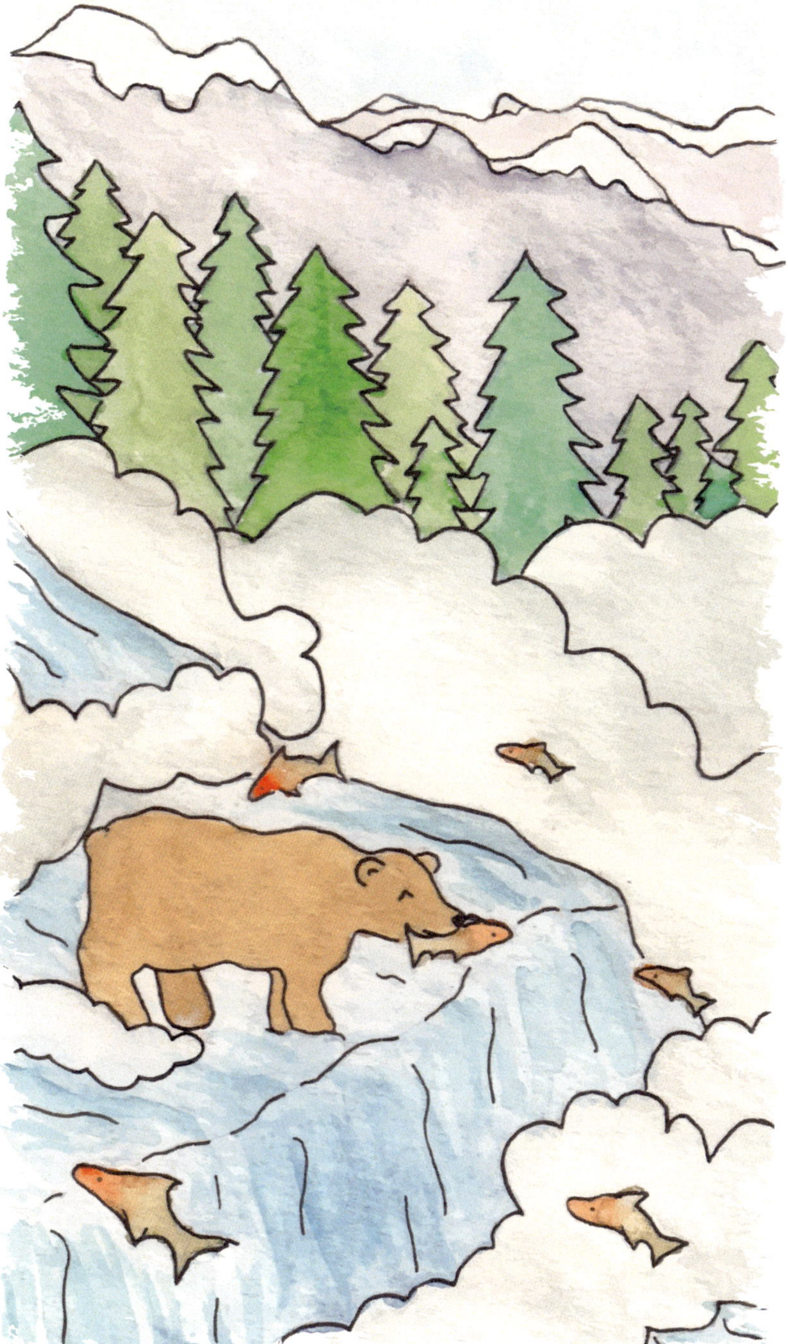

WHAT YOU BUILD IN YOUR MIND
MUST BE CLEARLY DEFINED
TO EVERY FINE DETAIL
YOUR FUTURE'S DESIGNED

THE ONLY WAY TO KNOW
IS IF YOU GO AND DO
WE WERE STUCK HERE ON THE GROUND
& THEN WE WENT AND FLEW

IF YOU HAVE PROTECTION
YOU'LL ALWAYS HAVE MORE FUN
IF SURROUNDED BY YOUR PALS
THEN YOU'LL NEVER HAVE TO RUN

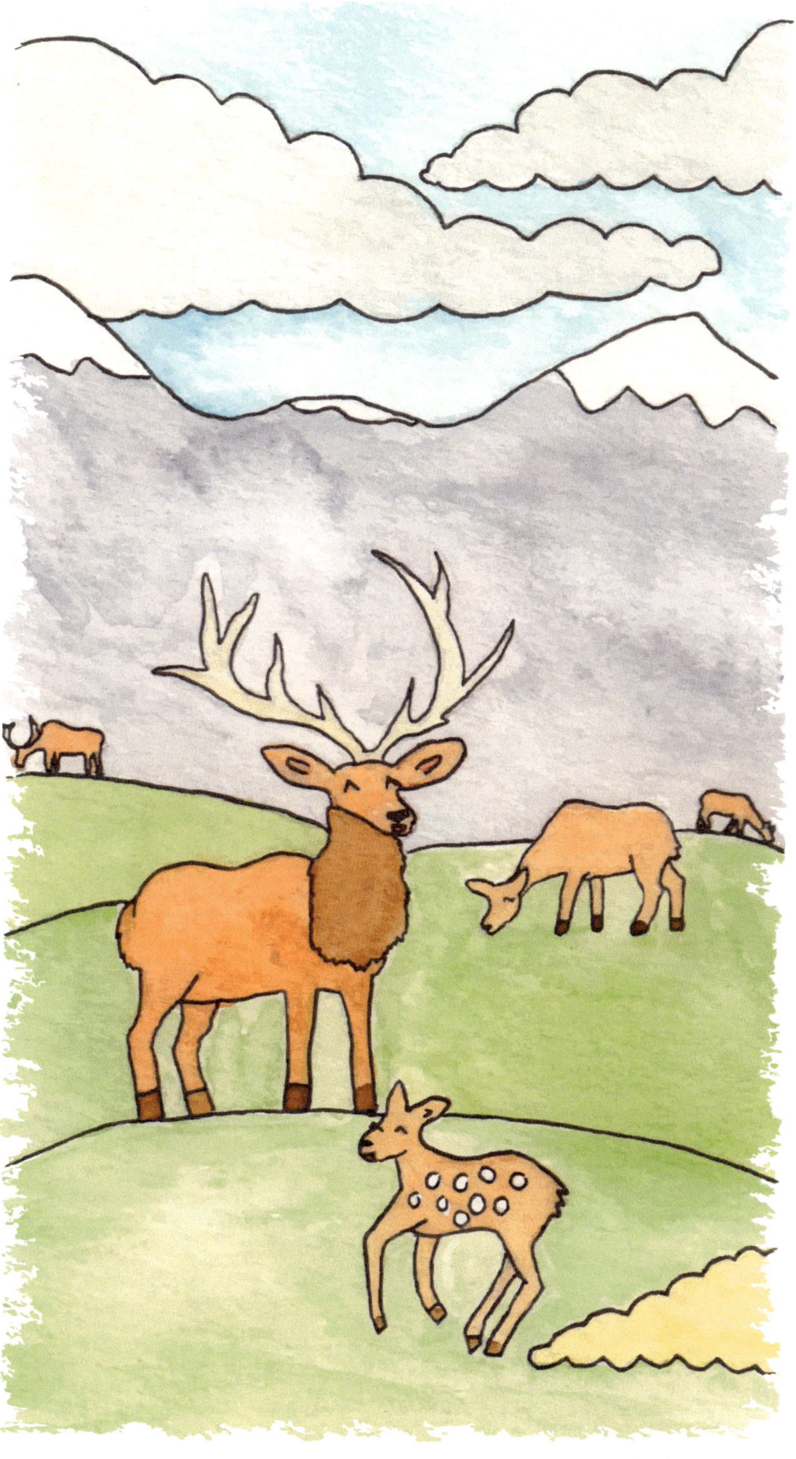

SELF-WORTH STARTS WITH YOU
YOU MUST CARE FOR YOURSELF
FOR ONE TO BE HAPPY
NOW THAT'S THE TRUE WEALTH

PEPPER IS TO SALT
WHAT KINDNESS IS TO JOY
FOR ONE WITHOUT THE OTHER
IS MUCH HARDER TO ENJOY

IF YOU WANT TO SPREAD THE LOVE
JUST START SIMPLE WITH A HUG
THE WORLD WOULD BE MUCH BETTER
IF ONLY KINDNESS WAS A DRUG

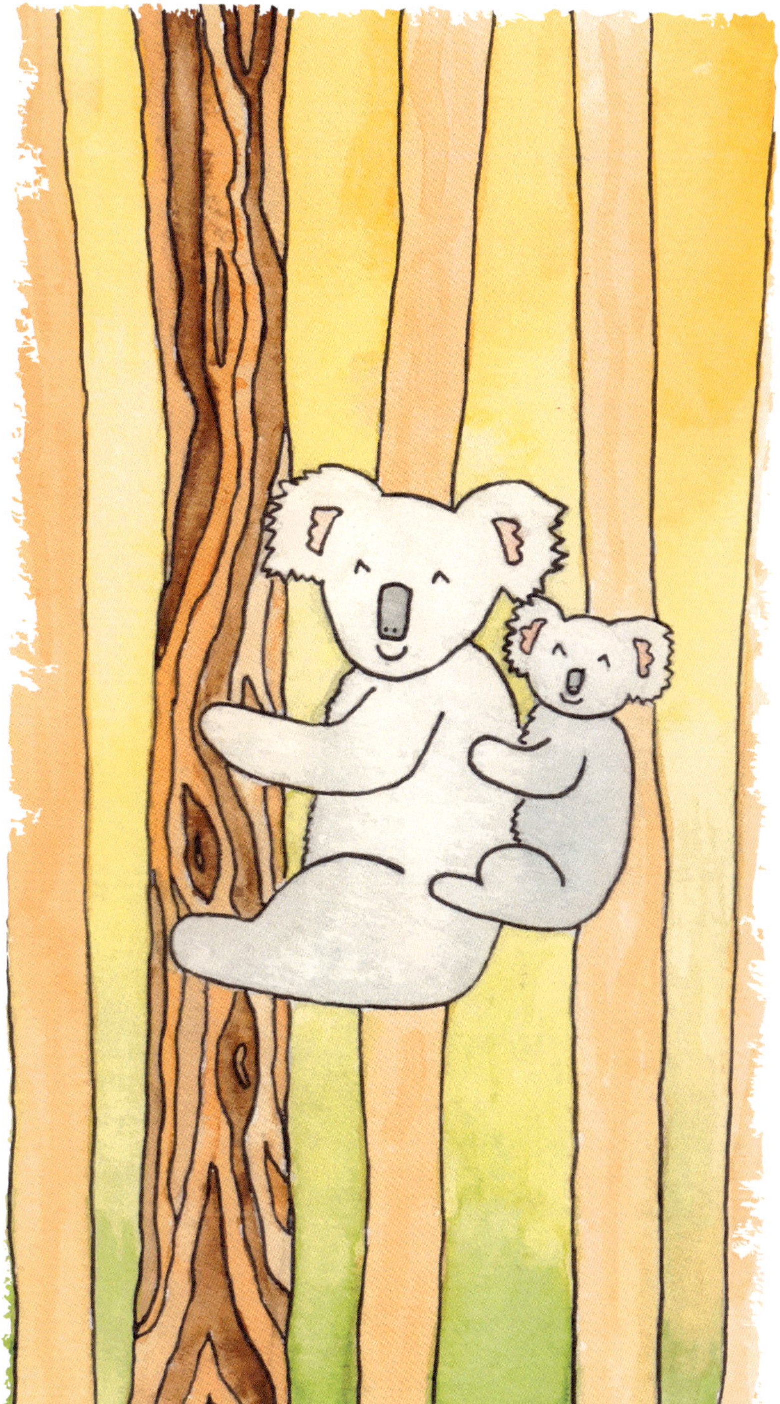

THERE'S ALWAYS MORE TO LEARN
TRUE SUCCESS IS WHAT YOU EARN
IF SOMETHING HOLDS YOU BACK
THEN THOSE BRIDGES YOU MUST BURN

A LIGHTER STARTS THE FLAME
& THEN IT'S YOURS TO TAME
WHAT GOOD IS ALL THIS POWER
IF YOU DO NOT KNOW YOUR AIM

EVEN WITH YOUR POWER
THERE'S NO NEED TO BE AGGRESSIVE
WE SHOULD QUIT WITH ALL THE PAIN
THAT'S BECOMING MORE EXCESSIVE

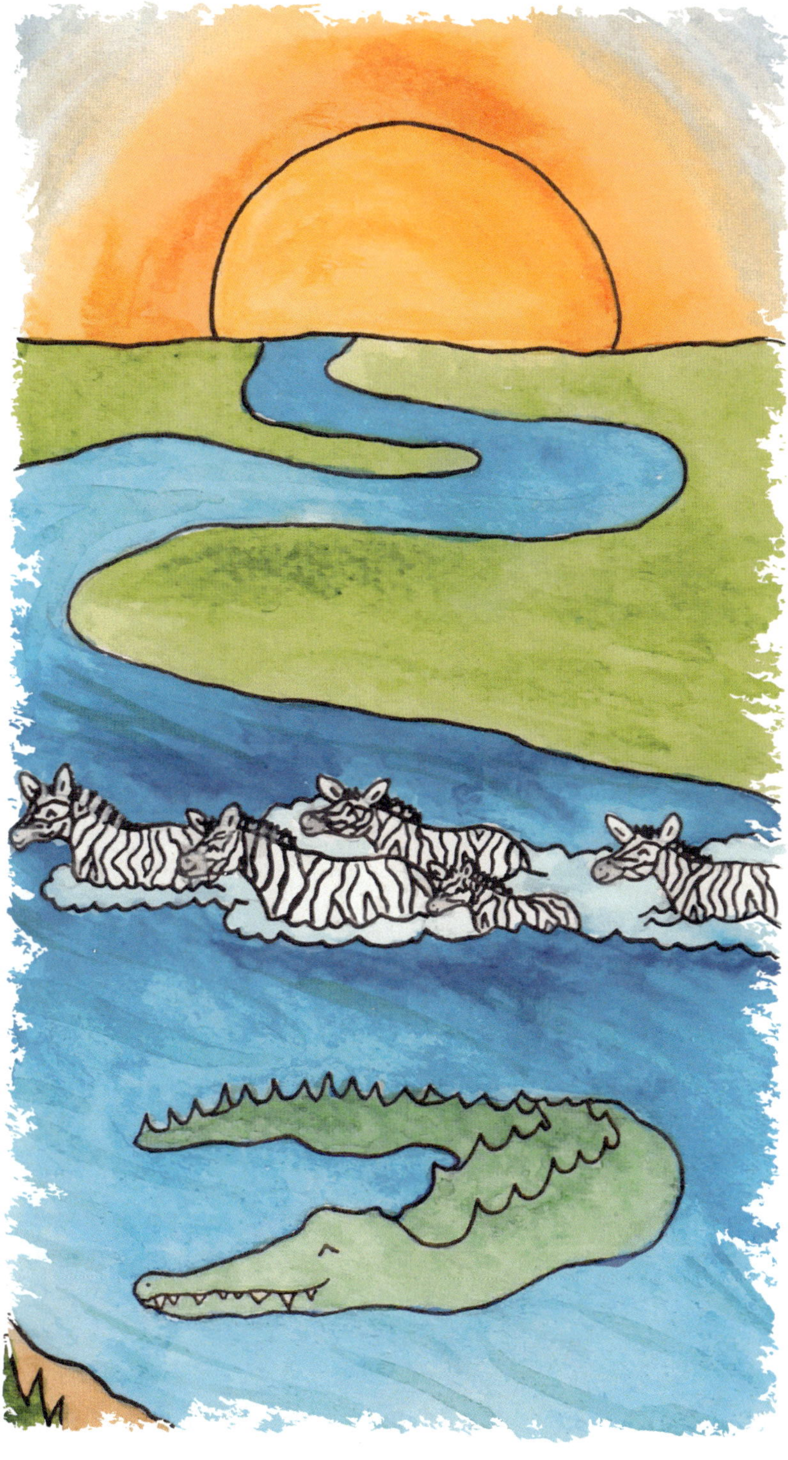

RAINBOWS FULL OF COLOR
THE DRIZZLE'S HIDDEN LOVER
YET THOUGH THEY SEEM AS SEPARATE
THEY'RE SO LOST WITHOUT THE OTHER

AS THE TREE IT GROWS WITH TIME
SOON BIG ENOUGH TO CLIMB
THE MOUNTAIN YOU ARE FACING
DISAPPEARS WITHOUT A SIGN

IT'S OKAY TO BE SAD
WHILE NOT STAYING TOO LONG
WE MUST STRIVE TO BE GLAD
IN A WORLD THAT IS WRONG